Just My Imagination

By Carson Jordan

Illustrations by Liopela

Just My Imagination

Hi, I'm Carson Jordan, and I am 10 years
old. Here's a little quote: " Never give up on
your dreams no matter what stops you!

I finally finished my book and
went to the bathroom.

To my surprise, I saw my twin brother and
dad brushing their teeth; they both looked
like bluefish. I stepped back and said, it's just
my imagination! It's just my imagination!

I ran to the polka dot kitchen to tell
my mom and big sister what I saw, and
there were two pink and purple monkeys
cutting up bananas for their cereal;

9

I stepped back and said, it's just my imagination! It's just imagination!

I stormed out and ran to the front door, yelling for my older brothers to come into the house, and there were two large lions with football jerseys running across the grass. I shut the door and stepped back, and said It's just my imagination! It's just my imagination!

13

I peeped around the corner and saw
my baby brother; he was a tiny kitten
drinking milk out of a green bowl.

I stepped back and said It's just my
imagination! It's just my imagination!

I ran so fast up the stairs to my
bedroom, shut the door

I looked in the mirror and noticed I was a
hairy wolf with a blue baseball cap, long
claws, and sharp teeth. I stepped back,
put my hands over my eyes, and said

It's just my imagination!
It's just my imagination!

— THE END —

Family is always important! ~ Carson J.

Worry is a waste of Imagination~ Walt

Let your imagination run wild, Be You! ~ Carson J.

"Everything that is real was imagined first".~ Velveteen Rabbit